I0015440

Legal Disclaimer

Table of Contents

FORWARD

Thank you for purchasing ***Getting Ready for a Presentation of Your New Business or Concept.*** The material within will give you a full blown Business Plan routine to follow. Not everyone will be ready for the full business plan, especially the financials. I will say that you will and should be able to prepare a good portion of the Business Plan which will serve to provide others with enough material to understand what you are trying to accomplish.

The Executive Summary will serve as a 1 to 2 page synopsis of the overall plan and it is a valuable piece of the whole to put together. The Executive Summary will give people enough material to decide whether they have interest in moving forward to see additional material or deciding that your project is not for them. Of course you can have others do all of this for you but it is a great experience to go through the process yourself and see your idea expand and crystalize. When I take you through the Elevator Pitch and Slide Show your project will continue to clarify and one should see clearly what you are trying to accomplish.

You are about to learn a **TON** as it relates to putting together your business package. No one will better know what you wish to accomplish better than you. No one can represent your idea with the same passion and sincerity as you. The results will be that the package reflects your personality and reflects your vision. You will save a lot of money. If you have no fear in writing your own material, then you will really appreciate this book. You can then do this routine for any project you do.

You will also learn a lot of new vocabulary and many concepts.

Enjoy the book and I will be waiting for you at the end as always.

Regards,

Louis

I. Things That Should Be in Your Business Plan.

Before we jump right into your business plan let me mention a few things. Not every business plan has to be compiled for the purpose of going in front of a venture capital type firm.

There are plenty of reasons to put together a business plan. For one, you want to go through the process because it helps you to clarify the concept as a whole. While you are going through the process of putting together each piece of your business plan, you will have new thoughts and revelations concerning the project that you had not yet considered. It forces you to slow down a bit, look at your industry a bit closer and to really decide whether you have something that is new and unique to the present offerings within that industry.

The business plan can be used in a bank, for a private investor, for an incubator group, for a group of friends who want to maybe back you and on and on. The longer you think about the concept, the more the concept will develop in terms of new twists, new things to overcome, and off shoots of the concept that you may have never even considered just a day ago so don't be in such a hurry. You will be surprised just how much information you will discover regarding your industry as you go through the process. Also, whatever you are working on, keep it under wraps to the best of your ability. You have to know when it is safe to bring the concept out in the open. I have authored a book entitled **Under Cover and Into the Light** which teaches you this very process of keeping the concept under wraps. It can be found on **www.lowcostempire.com**

Before and/or while you do your business plan, I urge you to grab the domain name of your choice and the same day lock up the social media with the same name so that all across the board, your proposed name is secure whether someone goes to Facebook, Twitter, Reddit, Tumblr, LinkedIn, Blogger, Pinterest, Instagram or any others. **Before you do this**, go to the **USPTO.Gov** data base and check that your proposed name is not already protected as a Trademark. Do the basic search and use different combinations of the proposed name and similar sounding names to see if there are potential problems/conflicts with your proposed name. If your proposed name is already protected and "**In Use**" by another person or entity, go back to the drawing board and I believe you will come up with the name that was meant for you. No point in using a name already protected or for that matter very close to a name already protected in all fifty states. I have authored a great book on filing your own Trademark, so if you want to do it yourself or get a really good feel for doing so, go to www.lowcostempire.com and look for "**Getting Down To Business, Filing Your**

First Trademark." But, what I will do now, is to give you a nice overview of the Trademark routine which will alert you to the importance of the Trademark. Don't Worry, I did not forget the Inventors. I have put together a book called *Low Cost Empire Vol. 2 – Getting Ready For A Patent Filing*.

II.   Mini Trademark Lesson

Do not underestimate the above question. The reason that you care about the trademark is for the following reasons. If the name you had hoped to use is **already trademarked**, meaning that someone else has the **sole right** to use that name in all 50 states, you would then want to seriously consider coming up with another name. The reason for going back to the drawing board is that the person or company already using that name **in that same line of business** (same international classification) as yours can legally sue you and effectively **prohibit you** from using the name anyway, so please don't waste your time. Simply go back to the "drawing board" and come up with another name. Chances are that the next one you come up with might be **unique** and you won't have to worry about any trademark issues. In order to search the trademark data base to see if your proposed business name/trade name is already secured and registered **by someone else**, you would go to http://www.uspto.gov and look for the "**Trademarks**" section as shown below:

Under **Trademarks** TRADEMARKS go to "Search and then Use the "**New User Search**".

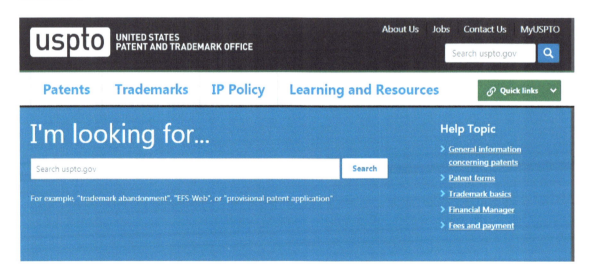

Learn about the process

Patents

General information concerning patents
Find out if a utility, design, or plant patent is right for you

Patent process overview
An overview of a patent application and maintenance process

Search for patents
Find existing patents, published patent applications and other published patent documentation

Trademarks

Trademark basics
What to know before you file an application

Trademark process
An overview of a trademark application and maintenance process

Search trademark database
Search for trademark applications and registrations with Trademark Electronic Search System (TESS)

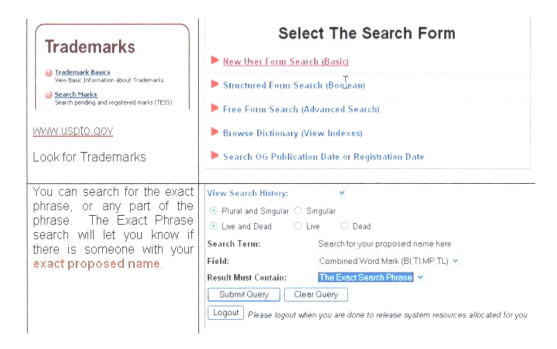

Now, if there is a match, check to see whether it is a "**live**" or "**dead**" filing. A dead filing simply means that the former owner did not file the appropriate documents and/or pay the required fees to maintain the trademark for whatever reason, and decided to **abandon** the trademark.

If it is a **dead filing**, you do not have to worry. The dead filings are marks that have been **abandoned** due to lapse of fees or the owner simply lost interest. If the search comes up with "**no hits**" then you can be sure to a high degree of certainty that the name is available for trademark protection. You can file on-line for a trademark by following the instructions carefully

If your initial search comes up clean (meaning no matches) then do the following. Search for any words of your proposed mark and see what comes up. Search for different uses or spellings such as **Car Fax** or **Kar Fax** or **Kids World** or **Kidz world (Example of Pseudo marks)**. Be as thorough as you can as a non-legal professional. If your name is for example **The World Group** search it out for **World Group, Our World Group, World Group Leaders etc.** Don't just get excited because there was not an initial direct hit.

Take your time and be thorough. If another filing is in the system, whether it be Pending **(TM)** or Registered ® the Trademark Examiner can determine that your particular filing is a bit too close to the already existing filing and can **reject** your application and you then lose $**400.00** hard earned dollars. **Do the work.** Be sure that your proposed mark is not already out there. Even if it is somewhat close you may have a problem, so don't do a lack luster job. **Search it out. Take a day or two to really search it out. Do the preliminary work before you file**. There is no need to lose your hard earned money. If it is already out there, then simply go back to the drawing board. I don't know about you, but I would rather have a **UNIQUE NAME** for a brand new venture that I came up with rather than a name that I **constantly** had to look over my **shoulder** because it is too similar to another name already in use.

The reason that I emphasize the trademark issue is because if you feel you have a great concept name, then moving for trademark protection is an extremely important step. If you think small you will simply stay small. Down the road, if you decide that you want to **Franchise** your business, you will need to "**own**" the rights to your name in all fifty states. The only way to achieve this is to be awarded a trademark. Another reason for needing a trademark is the **licensing** issue.

If, in the future, you find yourself wanting to enter into a licensing agreement, whereby an individual or company wants to **pay you for the right to use your name or logo** in some aspect of their business or to place your name or logo on some item like a cup, towel, clothing item, etc. then 1) you would only be in a position to enter into a licensing agreement if you did in fact **own the rights to the name and logo** under the classification of goods or 2) the classification of services that the prospective licensee is interested in. Otherwise, they don't need you and they would simply use that name or logo whenever they felt like it with no repercussions. For licensing, you have to get the book **Licensing Your Invention by Richard Stim**. He totally introduces you to the world of licensing. Go to **Amazon**, look for a used copy and you will truly get an education that will allow you to talk the talk from his user friendly book.

It is important to point out that you can apply for a trademark on-line www.uspto.gov and the website has **step-by-step instructions** concerning the filing. In my book, I go over the entire process with you from beginning to end with a lot more insight. If you have a brand new business and have not sold any goods or services across state lines then you can file what is called an "**Intent to Use**" Trademark Application. If from the moment you started your business you have been selling interstate (**commerce between states**), whether it is goods or services, then you can file an "**In Use**" Trademark Application. Again, these applications have built-in instructions. The filing fee is **$400.00**.

If you have filed an **intent to use application**, once your mark is deemed by the trademark examiner to be worthy of being granted, you then have **5 chances** to **renew** your **Intent to Use status** (6 month increments) before you must convert the status to **IN USE** or else you must forfeit the mark. **When you do convert over to an In Use application that will cost you $100.00. Note: If you initially file as In Use and submit your specimen from the start, you will have no reason to worry about the Intent to Use or the $100.00 dollar conversion fee. People who file the Intent to Use do so because they simply are not selling their item whether it be goods or services AS OF YET but they sure plan to.**

Each extension of an Intent To Use (**and you can do this five times**) will cost you **one hundred fifty dollars per extension**. As soon as you start to make sales from customers residing in another state you can then **convert your "Intent-To-Use" status over to "In-Use"** by filing your **In-Use** application.

Whether you file as **In Use** or **Intent To Use**, at a certain point, you will receive notice that you are going into the **Official Gazette** to see if there is any opposition. The Gazette is the Trademark magazine so to speak where the public gets the chance to see if there are any marks that are being proposed that clash with an already existing mark. If there is **NO OPPOSITION** from another already existing Trademark holder or someone with a current Trademark Application, you will receive a **Notice of Allowance after the 30 day period. [If you do get opposition concerning your Gazette listing, you will be notified from the Trademark Office]**. Once you issue your **Statement of Use**, if you had not done so from the beginning, approximately 3 months later, **your trademark will issue** and you are then protected in all fifty states against anyone using your name without your permission. Keep in mind that you don't have to already have the trademark in order to seek money. It would be great if you at least filed an application and you are somewhere within the chronology of the application.

Once you file for a Trademark you should be using the "™" symbol after your proposed name wherever and whenever you use it. The "™" symbol alerts people that although a Trademark has not yet been granted, it lets them know that you are claiming the name as yours and you are **currently somewhere along the chronology of the Trademark Application process**. If you are in the "service business" then use the "**SM**" superscripted after the name of your company or product name on your business cards, and other items bearing the name. When you are issued the Trademark and it becomes Registered, and is no longer just a pending application, you will then place a "®" at the end of the mark and you will make sure that it is on everything and everywhere that your name appears. The "®" symbol lets people know that the mark is your property, **protected in all fifty states from infringement** or unauthorized use. For those of you that think you are protected by simply placing a "™" after your trade name well you are not. **If you did not file an actual application then you placing a "™" after your trade name has no weight**. If someone should look you up in the database and see you are not in there, they can file for your mark and undercut you and thus take your mark.

Look at the list below and make an attempt to determine what international classification that your Trademark Or Service Mark will fall under. Also, do consider purchasing my book Low Cost Empire – Getting Down to Business – Filing Your First Trademark.

INTERNATIONAL SCHEDULE OF CLASSES OF GOODS AND SERVICES

GOODS

1. chemicals used in industry, science and photography, as well as in agriculture, horticulture and forestry; unprocessed artificial resins; unprocessed plastics; manures; fire extinguishing compositions; tempering and soldering preparations; chemical substances for preserving foodstuffs; tanning substances; adhesives used in industry.
2. Paints, varnishes, lacquers; preservatives against rust and against deterioration of wood; colorants; mordents; raw natural resins; metals in foil and powder form for painters, decorators, printers and artists.
3. Bleaching preparations and other substances for laundry use; cleaning, polishing, scouring and abrasive preparations; soaps; perfumery, essential oils, cosmetics, hair lotions; dentifrices.
4. Industrial oils and greases; lubricants; dust absorbing, wetting and binding compositions; fuels (including motor spirit) and illuminants; candles, wicks.
5. Pharmaceutical, veterinary, and sanitary preparations; dietetic substances adapted for medical use, food for babies; plasters, materials for dressings; material for stopping teeth, dental wax; disinfectants; preparations for destroying vermin; fungicides, herbicides.
6. Common metals and their alloys; metal building materials; transportable buildings of metal; materials of metal for railway tracks; non-electric cables and wires of common metal; ironmongery, small items of metal hardware; pipes and tubes of metal; safes; goods of common metal not included in other classes; ores.
7.Machines and machine tools; motors and engines (except for land vehicles); machine coupling and transmission components (except for land vehicles); agricultural implements other than hand-operated; incubators for eggs.
8. Hand tools and implements (hand-operated); cutlery; side arms; razors.
9.Scientific, nautical, surveying, electric, photographic, cinematographic, optical, weighing, measuring, signaling, checking (supervision), life-saving and teaching apparatus and instruments; apparatus for recording, transmission or reproduction of sound or images; magnetic data carriers, recording discs; automatic vending machines and mechanisms for coin operated apparatus; cash registers, calculating machines, data processing equipment and computers; fire extinguishing apparatus.
10. Surgical, medical, dental, and veterinary apparatus and instruments, artificial limbs, eyes, and teeth; orthopedic articles; suture materials.
11. Apparatus for lighting, heating, steam generating, cooking, refrigerating, drying, ventilating, water supply, and sanitary purposes.

12. Vehicles; apparatus for locomotion by land, air, or water.

13. Firearms; ammunition and projectiles; explosives; fireworks.

14. Precious metals and their alloys and goods in precious metals or coated therewith, not included in other classes; jewelry, precious stones; horological and chronometric instruments.

15. Musical instruments.

16. Paper, cardboard and goods made from these materials, not included in other classes; printed matter; bookbinding material; photographs; stationery; adhesives for stationery or household purposes; artists' materials; paint brushes; typewriters and office requisites (except furniture); instructional and teaching material (except apparatus); plastic materials for packaging (not included in other classes); playing cards; printers' type; printing blocks.

17. Rubber, gutta-percha, gum, asbestos, mica and goods made from these materials and not included in other classes; plastics in extruded form for use in manufacture; packing, stopping and insulating materials; flexible pipes, not of metal.

18. Leather and imitations of leather, and goods made of these materials and not included in other classes; animal skins, hides; trunks and traveling bags; umbrellas, parasols and walking sticks; whips, harness and saddlery.

19. Building materials (non-metallic); nonmetallic rigid pipes for building; asphalt, pitch and bitumen; nonmetallic transportable buildings; monuments, not of metal.

20. Furniture, mirrors, picture frames; goods (not included in other classes) of wood, cork, reed, cane, wicker, horn, bone, ivory, whalebone, shell, amber, mother-of-pearl, meerschaum and substitutes for all these materials, or of plastics.

21. Household or kitchen utensils and containers (not of precious metal or coated therewith); combs and sponges; brushes (except paint brushes); brush-making materials; articles for cleaning purposes; steel-wool; un-worked or semi-worked glass (except glass used in building); glassware, porcelain and earthenware not included in other classes.

22. Ropes, string, nets, tents, awnings, tarpaulins, sails, sacks and bags (not included in other classes); padding and stuffing materials (except of rubber or plastics); raw fibrous textile materials.

23. Yarns and threads, for textile use.

24. Textiles and textile goods, not included in other classes; beds and table covers.

25. Clothing, footwear, headgear.

26. Lace and embroidery, ribbons and braid; buttons, hooks and eyes, pins and needles; artificial flowers.

27. Carpets, rugs, mats and matting, linoleum and other materials for covering existing floors; wall hangings (non-textile).

28. Games and playthings; gymnastic and sporting articles not included in other classes; decorations for Christmas trees.

29. Meat, fish, poultry and game; meat extracts; preserved, dried and cooked fruits and vegetables; jellies, jams, fruit sauces; eggs, milk and milk products; edible oils and fats.
30. Coffee, tea, cocoa, sugar, rice, tapioca, sago, artificial coffee; flour and preparations made from cereals, bread, pastry and confectionery, ices; honey, treacle; yeast, baking powder; salt, mustard; vinegar, sauces (condiments); spices; ice.
31. Agricultural, horticultural and forestry products and grains not included in other classes; live animals; fresh fruits and vegetables; seeds, natural plants and flowers; foodstuffs for animals; malt.
32. Beers; mineral and aerated waters and other nonalcoholic drinks; fruit drinks and fruit juices; syrups and other preparations for making beverages.
33. Alcoholic beverages (except beers).
34. Tobacco; smokers' articles; matches.

SERVICES

35. Advertising; business management; business administration; office functions.
36. Insurance; financial affairs; monetary affairs; real estate affairs.
37. Building construction; repair; installation services.
38. Telecommunications.
39. Transport; packaging and storage of goods; travel arrangement
40. Treatment of materials.
41. Education; providing of training; entertainment; sporting and cultural activities.
42. Scientific and technological services and research and design relating thereto; industrial analysis and research services; design and development of computer hardware and software; legal services.
43. Services for providing food and drink; temporary accommodations.
44. Medical services; veterinary services; hygienic and beauty care for human beings or animals; agriculture, horticulture and forestry services.
45. Personal and social services rendered by others to meet the needs of individuals; security services for the protection of property and individuals.

END OF TRADEMARK MINI LESSON

III. Those who are Dealing with a Patent Device

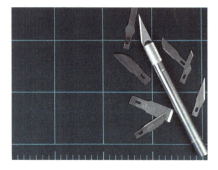

Again, I don't want to give you a book on how to get ready for a patent. If you go to lowcostempire.com, I have authored a book **Low Cost Empire Volume II, A Game Plan For Inventors**. That book gives you a strategy that you can follow which is thorough. I will give you a nice overview of what you can do concerning your patent before you go looking for money. Look, you are looking for money for one of the 3 usual things. Either you have a new concept such as a utility patent concept, a new business model or a service model or new device and you need some help getting it off the ground. The inventor not only has the Patent aspect to deal with, but they also have the marketing end, the production end and the Intellectual Property end in terms of a Trademark etc. so it is much more than I have a great idea. Today, in order to see real profit you have to be organized and you have to take steps to protect and preserve your rights over the ownership of the concept or product. So, even if you are not doing a patent, I suggest you still read this chapter since you will learn a lot regardless. So, here it goes.

I want you to learn the 1) **Chronology** of a **Utility Patent Filing**. 2) I want you to learn the basic checklist of how to check if **your proposed name of your invention is available** for ownership in the form of a **Trademark**. There is no reason why you should not simultaneously be pursuing a Trademark for your patent if you have a really good concept name. 3) Finally, I want you to learn about the world of **licensing**. All of this learning I want you to do over a period of 6 months to a year depending on how quickly you learn. The books that I will recommend are inexpensive but will quickly give you a **VERY CLEAR** understanding of the Patent process and the Licensing Process. You would rather pay a few dollars to have invaluable knowledge than to just hand your invention over to others and say do everything for me. You need to be in charge. You also need to be able to convey to others that you are in charge and there is no doubt about it. Otherwise, you set yourself to be taken for a lot of money and you will just end up being frustrated. So, if you think you truly have a good idea then you owe it to yourself and your family to really learn as much as you can so you can take part and feel comfortable when doing so.

Patenting can be expensive but sometimes it is necessary. So, before you get involved with this more complicated process, I would recommend the following. For one, go to **www.uspto.gov** or if you are not in the United States you can go to the Patent and Trademark database of your country and read everything you can on the patent process. Use the search feature in the Patent data base and start to probe and search for those inventions that are already patented or in the process of being patented in the same or similar subject area of your invention.

Use key search words that you feel would turn up your invention if it is already out there. The key words that you use will also help to bring up patents that are in the same ball park as your invention but maybe not exactly like your invention. **You want to know what is going on in the outside world. Search for your invention to the best of your ability. You want to see whether it is out there in any way, shape or form. Maybe certain aspects of your invention are out there but not the core of your invention**. Do your best but probe probe probe. At some point down the line you will have a Patent Search performed by a Patent Attorney but you are not there yet so do the work. By you doing the preliminary work, you are also learning the pieces of a patent and all of this will be invaluable to you!

Go to **Amazon.com** and purchase the book **Patent It Yourself** by **David Pressman**. I have had the pleasure of corresponding with Mr. Pressman and he is the real deal and a nice guy. I have filed **two Patents** using the Pressman book. The Pressman book is going to breakdown the **chronology of filing a patent from the beginning to the end**. It is an outstanding book for any beginner inventor. Go to **Inventorsdigest.com** where you will find all types of help. They are one of the best sources for **honest help** for new inventors. You will find mold makers, prototype people, electronic prototype people, graphic design people and other related services. I would recommend that you initially file a **Provisional Patent**. For a "Small Business Entity" which you are most likely to be, your cost will be $130.00 if you do it yourself. Add a few hundred dollars more if someone else does it for you.

A **Provisional Patent** will hold your conception date and **will give you up to a year to convert it over to a regular patent application**. Go to the USPTO.gov website and in the patent section look up the Provisional Patent Application. There are books on Amazon devoted to helping you file a Provisional application. The USPTO also has their own set of instructions. The

Pressman book also has a lot of info on the Provisional. The Pressman book will fill you in on what you need to know in order to file a Provisional Patent as well as the USPTO.gov site. The Pressman book will also provide you with a **very clear understanding of the entire Patent Application Process** and how each section is drafted and how it should look. This book is very friendly in terms of the writing style and takes what could be intimidating subject matter and makes it very easy to digest and understand. **If you are an inventor, then the Pressman book is your best friend**. You are going to use the Pressman book to learn the Chronology of the Patent Process, how each individual piece is drafted and how each piece of the patent application pertains to your invention. Richard Stim is the guy to go to for anything to do with Licensing. His books are great. Plenty of used copies on Amazon.

You may be excited about your new idea but be careful what you say. Telling others about your idea without the proper protection leaves you without any recourse if someone decides to tell others about your idea. Keep it under wraps for as long as possible. Learn as much as you can and do as much as you can by yourself. You should use **the need to know basis concept** when dealing with people. Use **Non-Disclosure/Non Compete Agreements** whenever you can. If possible, you want to get people (such as mold makers, prototypers etc.) to sign-off with a Non Disclosure at the very least that they will not divulge unnecessarily your information regarding your concept to others while you are in the process of seeking protection for your invention by having a patent granted. The Non-Disclosure might also include a small area for "**Work For Hire**" where not only do you want their silence but they should know that anything they prepare for you is your property. In other words, they should **not** have the ability to **show, email or display** materials they have prepared for you in terms of **drawings** or **electronic prototypes** without your permission and knowledge. Control the flow of information and be careful what you divulge.

You will know how much to say in each individual situation. You can talk in generality unless of course you are working with a known friend or your attorney. **Don't ever send your concept to anyone by mail or email** unless it is your attorney. Sending the invention out to someone you do not know is like handing them your concept. How can you possibly track who they show it to? Those invention companies that put in a supposed non-disclosure form and tell you to tell them your idea are in my mind bordering on criminal. They very well know that once you take the Jeanie out of the bottle that you are going to lose the ability to ever capitalize on the concept. What is even worse is the fact that no matter what you send, they will tell you it is amazing and hit you with a bill in order for them to do some water downed patent. STAY AWAY FROM THEM. When you are actually ready to do a real utility patent, you will go to a patent attorney and I can give you a great recommendation. In the meantime, file a provisional patent and that will buy you time in order to learn the necessary lingo and chronology so that you can properly take part in a very important part of your professional life.

I would suggest you go to **Google** or **Startpage.com** and start searching for **Non-Disclosure/Non-Compete Agreements**. When you find one that you like, tailor it to your situation. Make it very clear that you are coming to Joe Smith for prototyping services relating to my project in the field of _____. Don't be so general that the guy will not sign it since he works on technical things all the time. You want to get into his/her head that this is **"my project"** and don't even think about doing something that you will regret. Sometimes they will already have their own Non-disclosure documents but you should read them thoroughly before signing.

Join **LinkedIn.com** and look for groups that deal with your same subject matter. You are allowed to join up to **fifty** groups for free. Being involved with these groups will allow you to see what they are talking about concerning new technology etc. and you can make valuable connections in terms of manufacturers, financial people, marketers etc. If your idea is already out there then through your groups you will have a chance to see to what extent it is, by keeping a watch on your groups and their discussions and offerings. Pick your groups one by one. If you join a group and it is off the mark and not really what you need then simply leave that group and join another that might be closer to the subject matter of your invention.

If you wish to search the internet when working on your invention or for that matter anything that you wish to keep under wraps, then go to **startpage.com**. This site allows you to search without anyone else keeping track of what you are searching. If you feel you are breaking new ground then you want to operate in as stealth of a manner as possible. This site will allow you to do so without losing any searching capability. **Duckduckgo.com** is another search engine that protects your privacy.

IV. Putting Together Your Business Plan Piece By Piece

I am going to give you a very nice laundry list of those things that should be part of your business plan. After this, I will show you how to create an **Executive Summary** which is basically a nice synopsis of the business plan. When it comes to the business plan, I have seen many variations. So, I will at the end of this chapter, give you some places to go for business plans but sometimes it is good to take the best from a few plans and make an even better plan.

So, let us now go over those items that **should be** part of your business plan.

1. **Company Description** – In most cases you can briefly describe your company (a few sentences will do). Here is a sample:

Low Cost Empire is a line of business books covering everything from initial concept to open for business.

AdvanceTo Corporation is a legal training company that teaches top-tier style word processing for major law firms in New York City and around the world. AdvanceTo has thorough courses structured for the basic through the advanced user and can be given in person or over the internet.

2. **Legal Structure** – Depending on your type of corporation, inform us how your firm splits up the ownership responsibility, authority and liability. If the business happens to be a partnership, you need to explain the basic terms of your partnership so that a potential funding source understands who's responsible for what.

3. **Mission Statement**. Refers to the goals and objectives you could reasonably expect to accomplish. In a vision statement, however, those sorts of statements are more bold, and is looking at the project in its **most realized form** unlike where we are "**right now**." Some argue that vision statements don't belong in a business plan, but many investors want to know the entire picture that has been envisioned by the entrepreneur. So if you feel you have a compelling vision, let people know where you see this thing going.

4. **Describe the products or services** you intend to market. The product description statement should be complete enough so the reader has a clear idea of what you are actually attempting to bring to market. This might

mean discussing the product's application and end uses. You may want to point out any unique features or variations from concepts that can are currently on the market.

5.   **Proprietary Information**. The investor will be looking for any proprietary information (Patents, Trademarks, Copyrights) that will set your concept apart from the crowd, which is known as the **Unique Selling Proposition**, or ("USP"). Almost every business has one, whether it's a patented product or a unique marketing/promotional strategy like Federal Express and DHL when it absolutely and positively has to be there. Also having Intellectual Property **adds to the overall value of the project**. It also shows that you had belief enough in the project to make sure that it is properly protected.

6.   **Competitive Edge**. Be specific in showing how you will give your business a competitive edge. For example, your business will be better because you will supply a full line of products, unlike your competitor who only has a minimal product line. You're going to provide additional service after the sale; while your competitor does not provide support after the transaction is over. . Your merchandise will be of higher quality. You'll offer a money-back guarantee. You'll provide parts and labor for up to 90 days after the sale. So, explain your competitive edge to the best of your ability. What are you going to do that the others either will not nor can not do.

7.   **Factors That Will Make You Successful**. What factors will make you successful? Why do you think you can make a profit that way?" Just explain the factors that you think will make it successful (e.g., it's a well-organized business, it will have state-of-the-art equipment, its location is exceptional, the market is ready for it, it's an amazing product at a fair price, etc.). Factors that support your claims can be broad-in nature here; but, you can go into greater detail later. Talk about certain suppliers or experts you've spoken to about your business idea and how they responded to your idea. Your potential lenders may even ask you to clarify your choice of location or your reasons for selling this particular product.

8.   **Thoroughly Describe Your Product**. Describe your product in terms of several characteristics, including cost, features, distribution, target market, competition and production concerns. It's a good idea to use charts and tables as often as makes sense to quickly convey this information. Charts and pictures sometimes provide more information at a glance than going into some long drawn out explanation. **I will provide you with some good sample of PowerPoint slides that you may wish to use**. Show how you are going to position and promote your product.

9.   **What Is Your Unique Selling Proposition, or USP**. A product description is more than a mere listing of product features. You have to highlight your product's *most compelling characteristics*, such as low cost or uniquely high quality, that will make it stand out in the marketplace and attract buyers willing to pay your price. Features: Is your product faster, bigger, smaller or comes in more colors, sizes and configurations than others in the industry.

10.   **Who's Going to Buy and Why?** Even the best product must meet a need in the market—otherwise, it's just a curiosity, not a foundation for a business. So make sure your plan identifies your markets and potential customers and elaborates about why your potential customer is going to buy your product. Identify the market you're going after. Talk about your market in terms of its characteristics, its needs, *age groups, gender groups*, and if possible, its numbers. It is important to identify your market's size if possible. If you can point out that there are for example, more than 16 million users of a specific service or device in the United States, it will bolster your case

11.   **Licenses and Certifications**. Some paperwork is just paperwork, and some paperwork is essential. Every business must file tax returns, and most businesses must have certain licenses and certifications to do business.

Your plan should take notice, however briefly, of the fact that you have received or applied for any necessary licenses and certificates. If you don't bring it up, some readers will assume all is fine, while others may suspect the omission means you haven't thought about it or are having trouble getting the paperwork in order.

Aside from the usual *business licenses and tax forms*, there are any number of *certificates and notices* you may need. Owners of buildings must have their elevators inspected regularly, and in some cities they must post the safety inspection record publicly. Plumbers must be licensed in many states. Even City hot dog vendors have to be licensed by the city before they can offer their hotdogs to the public.

12.   **The State of Your Industry**. What is going on in your industry right now? What are the trends? What are the perceived problems? What are some of the new technology that is emerging? Look at your current trade magazines in your particular genre. What are they pushing? What problems are they talking about. Do you solve any of these problems? Are you considered state of the art?

13.   **Market Research**. The basic questions you'll try to answer with your market research include: Who are your customers? Describe them in

terms of **age, occupation, income, lifestyle, educational attainment, etc**. What do they buy now? Describe their buying habits relating to your product or service, including how much they buy, their favored suppliers, the most popular features and the predominant price points. Why do they buy? This is the tricky one, since you have to delve into consumers' heads. Some of the best market research is what you do on your own. This would include original interviews with consumers, published sources or perhaps competitive intelligence you've gathered on your rivals.

14.   **Trends**. Timing is everything. The best time to address a trend is at its start—or at least before it is widely recognized. If you can provide a business that satisfies an emerging market or new technology, you can generate growth that is practically off the scale. Use **tradepub.com** in order to find industry magazines to see the state of the art.

15.   **Overcoming Barriers to Entry**. If you want to become a semiconductor manufacturer, you'll need a billion-dollar factory or two. If you want to create a TV network, you'll need programming and affiliate stations in the major markets. These barriers to entry, exist to some extent in all industries. The barriers may be **monetary**, **technological**, **distribution** - or **market related**, or simply related to the ownership of prime real estate. An important part of analyzing your market is determining what the barriers to entry are. If the barriers are high, as is the case with airplane manufacturing, then you can be assured that new competitors are likely to be slow springing up. If they're low, as is the case with, say, self publishing, where anybody with a computer can take a shot, then you know there will be an endless supply of competition lured by the low investment and chance at easy bucks.

Be alert for **innovative competitors** (who may have an ingenious new method) while writing the section of your plan where you analyze barriers to entry. It may save you from a disastrous error, and will certainly demonstrate to investors that you've thought your plan through and are not jumping to conclusions. It will be very embarrassing to you if someone out there already has a much better mousetrap. It will look like you did not do your homework.

16.   **Pricing**. One of the most important decisions you have to make when preparing a business plan is what price to charge for what you are going to be selling. Pricing determines many things, from your profit margin per unit to your overall sales volume. It strongly influences decisions in other areas, such as the level of service you will provide and how much you will spend on marketing.

Pricing has to be a process you conduct concurrently with other tasks, including estimating sales volume, determining market trends and calculating costs. There are two basic methods you can use for selecting a price.

One way is to figure out **what it costs you altogether to produce or obtain your product or service, then add in a comfortable profit margin**. This markup method is easy, straightforward and, assuming you can sell sufficient units at the suggested price, guarantees a profitable operation.

It's widely used by retailers in particular. To use it effectively, you'll need to know **your costs** as well as **standard markups** applied by others in your industry.

The competitive pricing approach is more concerned with the competition and the customer. It looks at what your competition in the marketplace happens to charge, plus what customers are likely to be willing to pay, and sets prices accordingly. The second step of this process forces you to tinker with your own costs to yield a profit.

17.   **Distribution Concerns**. There are three main issues in deciding on a placement strategy: coverage, control and cost.

Cost, is an important part of any business decision, including distribution concerns. The other two issues, however, are unique to distribution, and a little more involved.

Coverage refers to the need to cover a **large** or **small** market. If you're selling paper towel, you may feel the need to offer it to virtually every household in America. This will steer you toward a conventional distribution scheme that runs from your paper towel factory to a group of wholesalers serving particular regions or industries to retailers such as grocery stores and finally to consumers.

What if you are reaching out to only a small group, such as head chefs of the top hotels in the country? In this case, the conventional, rather lengthy distribution scheme is clearly not viable. You're likely to do better by selling directly to the head chefs through a company sales staff, sales representatives, or perhaps an agreement with another company that already has sales access. In both these cases, coverage has a lot of influence on the design of your distribution system.

Control is important for many products. Certain lines of suits aren't sold at Target because the companies that make these garments work hard to control its distribution, keeping the costly apparel in high-end stores where its lofty prices can be sustained. Their need for control means that it deals only with distributors who sell to designer boutiques. Many manufacturers want similar control for reasons **of pricing, after-sale service, image and so forth**. If you need control over your distribution, it will powerfully influence placement decisions. You have to remember that if the essence of the company is going to take on an aura that it is above the norm, then you are going to have to monitor who gets to sell your product or service.

18.   **Who are Your Managers?**

Qualifications to run your business. You can provide this information by describing managers in terms of the following characteristics:

Education: If the credentials of the company managers are an impressive one, this can provide a strong reason for an investor or other plan reader to feel good about your company. Use your judgment in deciding what educational background to include and how to emphasize it. If you're starting a fine restaurant and your chef graduated at the top of his/her class from the Culinary Institute of North America, then emphasize that fact. If you're starting a courier service and your partner has an criminal justice degree from a little-known school, mention it but don't make a big deal out of it.

Employment: You can be proud to be an entrepreneur without feeling less than for initially working for somebody else. In fact, prior work experience in a related field is something many investors look for. If you've spent 10 years in management in the retail men's apparel business before opening a tuxedo outlet, an investor can feel confident that you know what you're doing. So describe **any relevant jobs you've had** in terms of job title, years of experience, names of employers, etc.

Skills: A title is one thing; what you learn while holding it is another. In addition to pointing out that you were a district sales manager for a furniture wholesaler, you should describe your responsibilities and the skills you honed while fulfilling them. For instance, note that you were responsible for hiring salespeople, planning and budgeting, working with key accounts, reporting to senior management and so on. **When you mention skills that you or your management team has, it reassures an investor that you can use them at your own company**.

Accomplishments: If one of your team members has been awarded patents, achieved record sales gains, or once opened an unbelievable number of new stores in the space of a year, now's the time to show those special achievements.

19.   Financials: Who Will You Be Approaching?

You may wish to mention in your business plan who you plan to approach. Most probably you are going to be looking at the 3rd column named outside sources. Most of you will be considering bank loans and or venture capital which include angel investors. No matter who you choose to help fund your company, many aspects of your company will already be in place and that will certainly help to develop a clear picture.

Check the sources you plan to approach for funding:

Personal Resources	Close-to-Home	Outside Sources
Savings	Friends	Bank loan
Second mortgage	Family	SBA loan
Insurance		Business credit card
Profit-sharing		Business credit line
		Venture capital
		Limited partnership
		Private offering

20.   Explaining the Financials.

INCOME STATEMENT

An income statement shows whether you are making any money. It adds up all your revenues from sales and other sources, subtracts all your costs, and comes up with the net income figure—also known as your bottom line. Income statements are called various names such as profit and loss statement, or P&L, and earnings statement are two common alternatives. They can get pretty complicated in their attempt to capture sources of income such as interest and expenses such as depreciation. But the basic idea is the following: If you subtract costs from income, then what you have left is your profit.

To compile your income statement, you need to know the following: Your gross revenue, which is made up of sales and any income from interest or sales of assets; your sales, general and administrative (SG&A) expenses; what you paid out in interest and dividends, if anything; and your corporate tax rate.

Low Cost Empire Volume 13

SAMPLE INCOME STATEMENT		
COOL SUN CORPORATION		
	YEAR 1	YEAR 2
Sales	$ 1,000,000	$ 1,500,000
Cost of Goods Sold	-750,000	1,050,000
Gross Profit	250,000	450,000
Operating Expenses	-200,000	-275,000
Operating Profit	50,000	175,000
Other Income and Expenses	3,000	5,000
Net Profit Before Taxes	53,000	180,000
Income Taxes	-15,900	-54,000
Net Profit After Taxes	$ 37,100	$ 126,000

BALANCE SHEET

If the income sheet shows what you're earning, your balance sheet shows what you're worth. Your balance sheet will help an investor see what valuable assets of the actual company that don't show up on the income statement, or that the company may be profitable but is heavily in debt. **The balance sheet will show everything your business owns**, and will subtract everything the business owes and shows the difference as the net worth of the business.

Accountants like to refer to the balance sheet in the following way. The things you own are called **assets**. The things you owe on are called **liabilities**. And net worth is referred to as equity.

The three elements are governed by this simple equation:

Liabilities + Equity = Total Assets

It can also be useful to look at it another way:

Assets – Liabilities = Net Worth

Both formulas mean the same thing.

A balance sheet shows your condition on a given date (**usually the end of your fiscal year**). Sometimes balance sheets are compared. That is, next to the figures for the end of the most recent year, you place the entries for the end of the prior period. This gives you a clean snapshot of how and in what ways your financial position has changed.

A balance sheet also places a value on the owner's equity in the business. When you subtract your liabilities from assets, what's left is the value of the equity owned by you and your partners.

Keeping an eye on this number will tell you whether you're getting richer or poorer.

SAMPLE BALANCE SHEET COOL SUN CLOTHING INC.	Year 1	Year 2
Assets		
Current Assets:		
Cash	$ 10,000	$ 20,000
Accounts Receivable	82,000	144,000
Inventory	185,000	230,000
Prepaid Expenses	5,000	5,0000
Total Current Assets	282,000	399,000
Fixed Assets:		
Land	0	0
Buildings	0	0
Equipment	15,0000	120,000
Accumulated Depreciation	-30,000	-30,000
Total Fixed Assets	120,000	90,000
Intangible Assets	0	0
Other Assets	10,000	11,000
Total Assets	$ **412,000**	$ **500,000**
Liabilities & Equity		
Current Liabilities:		
Notes Payable – Short Term	60,000	42,400
Current Maturities of Long Term Debt	30,000	30,000
Accounts Payable	82,000	86,000
Accrued Expenses	7,900	13,500
Taxes Payable	0	0
Stockholder Loans	0	0
Total Current Liabilities	179,900	171,900
Long Term Liabilities	120,000	90,000
Total Liabilities	$ 299,900	$ 291,900
Owners Equity:		
Common Stock	75,000	75,000
Paid-In-Capital	0	0
Retained Earnings	37,100	163,100
Total Owner's Equity	112,100	238,100
Total Liabilities and Equity	$ **412,000**	$ **500,000**

An asset can be anything of value that you own. It gets a little more complicated in practice, but that is the basic working definition. Assets come in two main varieties: current assets and fixed assets. *Current assets are assets that are easily liquidated or turned into cash*. They include cash, accounts receivables, inventory, marketable securities to name a few. Fixed assets include assets that take a bit more effort to turn into cash. *Examples are land, buildings, improvements, equipment, furniture and vehicles*. The fixed asset portion of the balance sheet sometimes includes a negative value that is a number you subtract from the other fixed asset values. This number is depreciation, and it's an accountant's way of systematically deducting the cost of a long-lived asset such as a building or piece of machinery or a car from your fixed asset value.

INTANGIBLES

Intangibles are another asset category. They include such things as patents, long-term contracts and a category called goodwill. Goodwill consists of things like the value of your reputation, which is not really susceptible to valuation. The best way to think of goodwill is like this: If you sell your company, the IRS says the part of the sales price that exceeds the value of the assets is goodwill.

Patents, trademarks, copyrights, exclusive distributorships, protected franchise agreements and the like do have somewhat more accessible value. They may never be turned into cash, but you can estimate their worth, or at least figure out what you paid for them and use that figure.

LIABILITIES

Liabilities are the debts your business owes. They come in two specific classes under the title **short term** and **long term**. Short-term also known as current liabilities are any debt that will be paid off within 12 months. This includes accounts payable (money you owe suppliers), short-term bank loans (shown as notes payable) and accrued liabilities you have built up for such things as wages, taxes and interest. Any debt that you won't be able to pay off in a year is long-term. Mortgages and bank loans with more than a one year term are placed in this class.

CASH FLOW STATEMENT

Where did the money go? The cash flow statement provides this answer. It monitors the flow of cash over a period of time such as *a year, a quarter or a month* and shows you how much cash you have on hand at the moment. The cash flow statement, also called the statement of changes in financial position, examines the changes that have occurred on the balance sheet. There are two parts to a cash flow statement: One follows the flow of cash into and out of the company, (cash flow statement) while the other shows how the funds were spent (statement of changes). The two parts are called, respectively, **sources of funds** and **uses of funds**. At the bottom is, naturally, **the bottom line**—called net changes in cash position. It shows if and by how much you have improved your available cash during the period.

SAMPLE CASH FLOW STATEMENT Coolsun Clothing Inc.		
Net Cash Flow From Operating Activities	**Year 1**	**Year 2**
Cash Received From Customers	$ 918,000	$ 1,438,000
Interest Received	3,000	5,000
Cash paid to suppliers for inventory	(853,000)	(1,091,000)
Cash paid to employees	(80,000)	(120,000)
Cash paid for other operating expenses	(69,300)	(104,400)
Interest paid	(17,800)	(15,000)
Taxes paid	(15,900)	(54,000)
Net cash provided (used) by operating activities	($ 115,000)	$ 58,600
Net Cash Flow From Financing Activities:		
Additions to property, plant and equipment	(150,000)	0
Increase (decrease) in other assets	(10,000)	(1,000)
Other investing activities	0	0
Net cash provided (used) by investing activities	($ 160,000)	($ 1,000)
Net Cash Flow Financing Activities:		
Sales of Common Stock	75,000	0
Increase (decrease) in short-term loans (includes current maturities of long-term debt)	90,000	(17,600)
Additions to long-term loans	120,000	0
Reductions of Long Term Loans	0	(30,000)
Dividends paid	0	0
Net cash provided (used) by financing activities	$ 285,000	$ (47,600)
Net increase (decrease) in cash	$ 10,000	$ 10,000

PERSONAL FINANCIAL STATEMENT

Investors and lenders look for business plans with substantial investments by the entrepreneur, or an entrepreneur who is personally guaranteeing any loans and has the personal financial strength to back those guarantees. Your personal financial statement shows business plan readers how you stack up financially as an individual. *If you don't initially have a lot money to put in a project depending on your FICO score, you can get Business Lines of Credit, you can do a Term Loan, you can try raising money through crowd funding, affiliation, private label marketing, or doing something that may not have to do with the current project but raises money nevertheless.* Having raised some money is better than nothing. It does go to show that you have made an effort so some fund raising effort is better than none.

A typical personal financial statement comes in two parts. One is similar to a company balance sheet and lists your liabilities and assets. A net worth figure at the bottom, like the net worth figure on a company balance sheet, equals total assets minus total liabilities.

A second statement covers your personal income. It is similar to a company profit and loss statement, listing all your personal expenses such as rent or mortgage payments, utilities, food, clothing and entertainment. It also shows your sources of income, including earnings from a job, income from another business you own, child support or alimony, interest and dividends, and the like.

The figure at the bottom is your net income; it equals total income minus total expenses. If you've ever had to fill out a personal financial statement to borrow money for a car loan or home mortgage, you've had experience with a personal financial statement

BREAK-EVEN POINT

One of the most important calculations you can make is figuring out your break-even point. This is the point at which your revenues equal costs. Knowing your break-even is important because when your sales exceed this point, you begin to produce profits. When your sales are under this point, you are still losing money.

FINAL PIECES OF THE BUSINESS PLAN – THE APPENDIX

KEY EMPLOYEE RESUMES

The management section of your business plan will contain a listing and brief descriptions of the senior managers and other key employees on your team. However, many investors and lenders are going to want to know more about you and your important associates than you give them in that section. To show the strength of your team, you can include full resumes in an appendix.

PRODUCT SAMPLES

If your products are portable enough, you may be able to include samples in your appendix. Some examples of products that may be included in your business plan are fabric swatches, stationery samples, printing samples, or screen shots and maybe links that show an electronic prototype showing the item in action so to speak.

It's important not to overdo it with product samples. Investors tend to regard many entrepreneurs as being somewhat more product-focused than operations - or marketing-minded. You can provide samples if it's feasible and helpful. But don't expect great samples to overcome any deficiencies in the concept, management, marketing, operations or financing presented in your plan.

PRODUCT PHOTOS

Appendices are good places to include photographs of products you have to see it so to speak because it may be difficult to explain in words. It is acceptable to include line drawings of products in the main sections of your plan. But again, most investors are more interested in such items as your balance sheet, management experience and cash flow projections than they are in glossy product photos.

ADVERTISING SAMPLES

It may be smart to include examples of the advertising you intend to use to market your products or services. For many companies, innovative and persuasive advertising approaches are essential to their success. Without actual examples of the ads, it may be difficult for readers to grasp the appeal and power of your marketing ideas. A lot of the funding people have marketing know how so they may appreciate your advertising samples.

Copies of newspaper and magazine ads, photos of billboards, still photos from TV spots, online ads and transcripts of radio spots are all acceptable. However, keep in mind that this information is optional. If you have an uninspired advertising campaign, it won't help you to expose investors to that fact.

PRESS CLIPPINGS

Reviews and articles in influential publications and broadcast shows drive many product sales. If your new concept just got rave reviews in a major trade magazine, by all means put in here for all to see. You may also want to include complimentary ratings, certifications or other endorsements by entities such as travel guides, associations, and watchdog groups. If your restaurant received an impressive number of stars from a popular rating guide, you should mention that as well. Good press is always valuable.

SOME PLACES TO OBTAIN BUSINESS PLANS:

Score.org – Under their "Templates and Tools" section they have business plan templates.

Entreprenuer.com
www.entrepreneur.com/formnet/businessplantemplates.html

V. The Executive Summary

The Executive Summary serves as a snapshot of your business plan and enables one to get a very good feel of your project by viewing this document. Based on what they see in the Executive Summary goes a long way at whether an investor decides they would like to see more. What we want to do is to have an Executive Summary that does not inundate the reader with info but comfortably gives the reader a very good and concise overview of the project. The goal of this chapter is to show you a few types of executive summary samples.

I am going to go over two types that I have personally participated in. In the first one, I blacked out some sensitive areas, but you will clearly get the point of what can be in the Executive Summary. The first one I chose to show because it is a bit too long but does show the **gamut** of what can be included. The only thing I left out on the first one was a short synopsis of the team but there is a lot of information in the first one so that you will clearly understand what an Executive Summary looks like and how it is put together. I will unfold it for you in piecemeal.

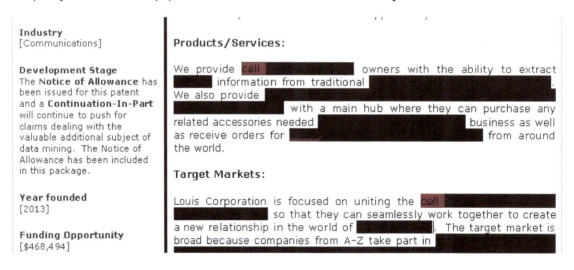

LOUIS® INTERACTIVE
Executive Summary
[A site to remember]
US Patent No.:
TRADEMARK REGISTRA
Copyright 2014 © by Louis Ell

Contact Information
Louis Corporation
Louis Ellman, President

Anywhere Avenue
Any City, State Zip
LawFirm: YOUR LAW FIRM,
located in City of Law Firm,
New York

Business Description:

The Mission of this corporation is to be the catalyst and liaison between the ▮▮▮▮ Companies, ▮▮▮▮ and ▮▮▮ Companies. The three industries need to work in conjunction for the purpose of giving people the opportunity to *easily secure* ▮▮▮▮ related directly to an ▮▮▮▮ for ▮▮▮▮. A "▮▮▮▮" is all that is needed to ensure that you don't lose out on an opportunity.

1.   Here is the top portion of the Executive Summary. **Note:** A) I placed the name of the company, B) the Patent Number associated with it, C) my Trademark Registration Number and D) I am claiming Copyright for the textual portion of the Executive Summary. You may not have your Patent or Trademark at the time of writing your Executive Summary but you may have them pending or somewhere along the chronology and you can put that information down. In the tan area to the left note that I have placed 1) my contact information, 2) my title, 3) my address and 4) the name of the law firm that I am using or plan to use. Under **"Business Description"**, I tried to put in a nice concise mini-summary of the proposed business. If you don't have Intellectual Property fill out the top portion of the Executive Summary.

Industry
[Communications]

Development Stage
The **Notice of Allowance** has been issued for this patent and a **Continuation-In-Part** will continue to push for claims dealing with the valuable additional subject of data mining. The Notice of Allowance has been included in this package.

Year founded
[2013]

Funding Opportunity
[$468,494]

Products/Services:

We provide ▮▮▮▮ owners with the ability to extract ▮▮▮▮ information from traditional ▮▮▮▮. We also provide ▮▮▮▮ with a main hub where they can purchase any related accessories needed ▮▮▮▮ business as well as receive orders for ▮▮▮▮ from around the world.

Target Markets:

Louis Corporation is focused on uniting the ▮▮▮▮ so that they can seamlessly work together to create a new relationship in the world of ▮▮▮▮. The target market is broad because companies from A-Z take part in ▮▮▮▮

2.   So moving right along, we have the **"Products/Services"** section and a short paragraph on the **"Target Markets"** that your new device, patent or

service will serve. If you look to the tan area on the left we have a title called "**Industry**" followed by another title called "**Developmental Stage**". If you notice in this area, for this particular Executive Summary, that I gave them up to date information concerning the issuance of my patent for the device that I was seeking funds for at the time. We then have a title called "**Year Founded**" and you can put the year you were incorporated if you are incorporated. The title "**Funding Opportunity**" you will put the total amount of money you are seeking. Then underneath, you do a short synopsis (breakdown) of what you are going to be using the money for.

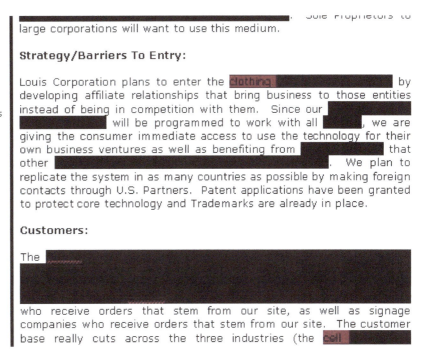

Use of Funds
$100,000 Product Development
$225,000 Marketing/Sales
$18,030 Domain and TM Protection
$4,000 Worldwide Affiliate Program
$50,000 Licensing agreements for Trademark Use
$25,000 for Travel

Existing Investors
The Process has begun.

large corporations will want to use this medium.

Strategy/Barriers To Entry:

Louis Corporation plans to enter the ▇▇▇▇▇ ▇▇▇▇▇▇▇▇▇▇▇▇ by developing affiliate relationships that bring business to those entities instead of being in competition with them. Since our ▇▇▇▇▇▇▇▇▇▇ will be programmed to work with all ▇▇▇▇, we are giving the consumer immediate access to use the technology for their own business ventures as well as benefiting from ▇▇▇▇▇▇▇ that other ▇▇▇▇▇▇▇▇▇▇▇▇▇▇▇▇. We plan to replicate the system in as many countries as possible by making foreign contacts through U.S. Partners. Patent applications have been granted to protect core technology and Trademarks are already in place.

Customers:

The ▇▇▇▇▇▇▇▇▇▇▇▇▇▇▇▇▇▇▇▇▇▇▇▇▇▇▇▇▇▇▇▇▇ who receive orders that stem from our site, as well as signage companies who receive orders that stem from our site. The customer base really cuts across the three industries (the ▇▇▇▇▇

3.   Moving right along, we have a title called "**Strategy/Barriers To Entry**". Here, you will attempt to summarize how you enter the market and how you can overcome any hurdles. You also want to show how you plan to do it smoothly and express your idea of how you will enter the market in the most cost efficient way that affords the least amount of resistance to you and your wallet (in essence, your strategy). Next, we have the "**Customers**" section and you can identify what you feel is the profile of your would-be customer. In the tan section to the left, we have the very important "**Use of Funds**" section where you do a quick breakdown of the money as to where you plan to allocate it. The "**Existing Investors**" section you **may** or **may not** wish to use it. You may not feel comfortable letting other people know who already committed money. The reason for this is that if your Executive Summary gets into the wrong hands, they can then approach your investor(s) and attempt to **name drop** saying that they

know you and they too are looking for money. In this particular Executive Summary, I was honest and I simply said that the process has begun meaning I don't have any investors as of yet. You may wish to say under the Existing Investor section "**to be supplied**" so you don't give that up unless you feel that you have a serious investor and you are past the informal aspect of dealing with a particular group.

Competition:

Of course we will have competition, but we believe that with our business model it will not be hard to come by customers, since we are giving business to those who fill orders for us. Just as the world of ▓▓▓▓▓▓▓ cannot be owned by one entity, this new medium will also be too big to control exclusively, but we know that we will be able to control a fair share and should be able to have a significant share in the United States and countries around the world. Our brand recognition will help to keep our customer base climbing in an upward trend. As

Competitive Advantage:

We believe that our competitive advantage is that we are not producing anything, in essence. We are acting as a hub. There is no shortage of qualified ▓▓▓▓▓▓▓▓▓▓▓▓▓▓▓▓▓▓▓▓▓▓▓▓▓▓▓▓▓▓▓▓▓▓ in the United States and around the world. We are not affected by costs pertaining to running a ▓▓▓. If you think about it, we are actually creating the industry, that is to say, the bringing together of the ▓▓▓▓▓▓▓▓▓▓▓▓. By Louis Corporation acting as a hub we help to standardize the industry and stay in the forefront as it relates to new developments. Since we are not relying exclusively on our patent, we have the flexibility to go with the flow and make use of any new

Explanation for the Amount of Funding:

The amount asked for, $468,494, we believe would allow us to accomplish the following: as a first round of financing, it would allow us to have applications created for all ▓▓▓▓▓▓▓▓▓▓▓▓▓▓▓▓ ▓▓▓▓▓▓▓▓▓▓▓▓▓▓▓▓▓▓▓▓▓▓ ▓▓▓▓▓▓ to be used for certain situations, such ▓▓▓▓▓▓▓▓▓▓, etc. We will be able to experiment and create the standard. The money will also be used for

4.   Above, we have the "**Competition**" section and you should give a short but concise overview. Remember, you will expand heavily in your business plan so do a nice and concise job in the Executive Summary. The same thing for your "**Competitive Advantage**" section. Give a taste of what will place you in a great position to compete with the current companies that are already

participating in the proposed line of business. Finally, in your "**Explanation for the Amount of Funding**" section if you should so choose to use it (**you may wish to just go with the info you already have in your left side panel**) just give a concise synopsis with a bit more info than shown in the left side panel.

Business Model:

The Louis business model is based off of affiliate relationships, whereby Louis Corporation does not have to ███. We will also be part of affiliate programs where website owners who are in the three lines of business that we will be dealing with will be able to place our banners on their site, which will exponentially expose our business all over the world. █████████████████ ██████ "

Distribution/Sales Model:

Our customers will be serviced by proven companies that are already up and running and profitable for some time. ██████████████ ████████████████ will not have to re-tool in any significant fashion. Everything that will be sold on the Louis site will be produced and sent

5.   For the "**Business Model**" section, attempt to do a quick summary concerning the type of business model you will be attempting to employ. Are you local and global, are you internet based, do you actually manufacture or are you totally affiliate related etc. For the "**Distribution/Sales Model**" section do a concise paragraph on how your will get your product or service into the hands of your would-be customer.

Technologies/IP:

We have Trademark Protection and have been awarded our Patent.

6.   Finally, under the "**Technologies/IP**" section let the investor know what you have done, are doing or plan to do in terms of protecting the name of the product or service, the Patents that have or will issue if you have a device or new disruptive business model etc. The intellectual property is important to a would-be investor because it gives value to the project. By things being protected by Trademark or Patent it simply means that you will own those items and other entities have to approach you for the legal use of those items. The

items that are protected add overall value to the company and have **brand recognition** and **licensing value** as well.

ONE MORE SAMPLE OF THE EXECUTIVE SUMMARY:

The first Executive Summary that I went over with you was one where I had a patented device that I was attempting to get funding for. The present situation concerns a gold mine in Mexico that is available for sale. So, let us see how we broke this one down:

GOLD·MINES¶

- We·are·offering·for·starters·a·120·hectare·gold·mine.¶
- ·My·Mexican·counterpart·**Name· of· Individual**·is·in·the·business·of·Import·Export.··He·also·has·experience·in·running·a·mine.··He·has·direct·access·to·approximately·50·plus·mine·owners.¶
- The·mine·owners·trust·Mr.·Guzman·as·a·local·and·as·a·advocate·for·them·to·assist·them·in·obtaining·JV·capital·and/or·people·or·mining·companies·that·have·interest·in·purchasing·the·mines·outright.¶
- All·of·the·mines·have·their·own·workers·who·are·loyal·to·the·particular·mine·owner.··The·overall·plan,·would·be·to·activate·the·mines·one·by·one·and·be·in·a·position· to· sell· the· gold· at· a· discount· that· would· be· fair· and· inviting· to· prospective·gold·buyers.··I·am·in·a·position·whereby·I·know·gold·buyers·who·are·interested· and· capable· of· buying· large· quantities.···I·know·people·in·the·gold·industry·that·can·assist·me·in·putting·together·a·proper·FCO·or·SCO·in·order·to·provide·a·prospective·Gold·Buyer·with·what·is·being·offered.¶
- There· are· mining· companies· looking· around· and· contacting· the· owners· of·mines·but·we·feel·that·we·have·a·good·chance·since·Mr.·[name·of·person]·is·a·local·and·we·are·not·looking·to·pay·bare·minimum·to·the·mine·owners·as·many·of·the· mining· companies· do.·· We· feel· that· we· can· offer· them· a· fair· deal· and·have·plenty·of·room·to·make·profit.¶

Contact·Information↵
Louis·Ellman↵

Industry↵
Gold·Mining¶

Development·stage↵
For·Sale¶

Purchase·Opportunity↵
[$2,500,000]¶

Type·of·Mines·Available↵
Gold,·Silver·and·Copper¶

Existing·Debt↵
[$0]¶

1.   Take a look at this particular executive summary. Notice that it gets right into what they have to offer, in this case a property that is a gold mine. This particular executive summary acts as both an Executive Summary/Partial Business Plan. In the left hand side, we have the contact info, the industry, the amount of money being asked for the property and we threw in the fact that the property has no existing liabilities.

Low Cost Empire Volume 13

Investors↵
Buy/Lease¶

Ask↵
Ask·us·for·our·NDA·and·
Buyers·side·Finders·
Agreement×

OPPORTUNITY·¶

↓→ The· mine· that· we· wish· to· offer· first· has· a· higher· density· of· gold· than· normally·found·in·3·of·the·drill·points.··In·fact,·many·of·the·mines·that·we·will· be· offering· have· high· density· samples· in· comparison· to· many· other· mines· being·grabbed·by·investors·and·mining·companies.··What·we·like·about·the· first·mine·is·that·it·is·the·following:··¶

↓→ 1)·It·is·close·to·roads,·2)·close·to·the·home·of·the·mine·owner·and·3)·very· close· to· a· Gammon· Lake· Gold· Processing· Plant.··To· comfortably· get· this· particular· mine· up· and· running· we· would· need· an· investment· of· approximately·$150-200·thousand·US·Dollars.··That·would·allow·us·to·rent· equipment·and·give·the·mine·owner·an·initial·deposit·that·he·has·requested· to·show·that·we·are·serious.··We·will·be·able·to·provide·the·current·permit· for·this·mine.··¶

↓→ The· goal· would· be· to· get· the· money· back· to· the· investor· plus· _____· commission·and/or·a·percentage·of·the·take·as·a·partner.··¶

↓· Once· the· money· is· paid· back· with· the· interest· and/or· percentage· overall· profit·we·would·want·to·utilize·this·same·routine·again·for·the·next·targeted· mine.¶

↓→ At·first,·we·would·be·receiving·cash·for·the·gold.··This·would·be·_____·per·oz· from·the·Gammon·Lake·gold·processing·facility·which·is·close·by·to·the·first· mine·in·question.¶

↓→ The·overall·goal·would·be·to·create·a·processing·plant·of·our·own·preferably· across·the·US·Border·or·to·utilize·an·existing·plant·so·that·we·can·process·the· gold·and·create·bullion·bars·and/or·dore·bars.··If·we·followed·this·routine·an· initial·investment·of·let·us·say·$200,000·can·be·paid·back·and·utilized·again· and·again·in·order·to·bring·the·next·mine·on-line¶

↓→ Each· mine· would· have· a· separate· contract· with· the· mine· owner· clearly· stating·the·profit·share·of·the·mine·owner·vs.·each·individual·involved·with· each·individual·mine.··The·goal·would·be·to·at·any·one·time·to·have·20·mines·

2.   Now under the heading of **"Opportunity"** we have listed all of the good attributes associates with this opportunity. On the left side panel we have alerted the investors that the mine can be bought outright or leased. We also have an NDA (Non-Disclosure Agreement) and an agreement for the Buyer's side which will make sure that we are all on the same page in terms of non-circumvention and clarity as to commissions for the brokers associated with the sale.

BENEFIT¶

The mines that we have available will place a new source of gold, silver and copper mines on the market for sale or lease. There are companies starting to snoop around but the locals know that any deal from an outside source will be the minimal offer in comparison to Mr. _____ who will give a more competitive offer. Being that Mr. _____ is a local, I believe we have the advantage and ultimately can win any debate on who to work with. Mr. _____ has known mining companies to come in and take multiple tons of earth with 4-5 grams per ton and hand the miner a few hundred dollars so we feel we can do better.¶

COMPETITION¶

The group of mines that we have for sale span across three states in Mexico. There is no long broker chain just myself and Mr. _____ who is the connection to the actual mine owner(s). This is an opportunity to buy one mine or a large group of mines. What we have to offer can provide a mining company or investor with a significant new source of gold that places them in a position for either ownership or temporary control for a fixed period of time. It is also important to note that each mine has a pool of available workers. Mr. _____ has a good relationship with people in the American Consulate and provide good references as needed.¶

INFORMATION¶

- Most of the mine owners are also farming people without significant monetary resources.¶
- In terms of information for each mine, we will have a lab report, maps and proof of ownership and permits for the mine. It would be up to the investor if he wishes to do a 43-101 or send an engineer to the site for independent testing and analysis.¶
- They (mine owners) as well as Mr. _____ expect that the potential buyer or investor will want to send a representative to view and sample the mine for confirmation of the provided lab report from our side.¶
- My contact will make such a meeting possible and will act as a guide as well as the connection to the locals who trust him.¶

OTHER POSSIBILITIES¶

Initially, we can have the gold processed locally and be paid locally. We have discussed the possibility of creating a refinery that 1) can locally serve the mines in that area, 2) establish or utilize a refinery across the border and traffic the unprocessed gold securely to the refinery location. If even 20 of the fifty are operational, a significant ongoing gold selling opportunity will arise. You just have to do the math to realize the amount that can be generated if the mine owners participated in a consortium.×

3.   Moving right along, I take care of the **"Benefits"** section and the **"Competition"** section and provide a concise but short paragraph. I then follow up with an **"Information"** or **"Facts"** section that I felt the possible buyer would appreciate knowing. It might also help to make the sale.

4.   Finally, I include an **"Other Possibilities"** section. Here I try to look further up the road give a broad vision of where it could go.

With the two samples of the **"Executive Summary"** that I have gone over with you I now believe you will be comfortable putting one together. I think you should first put together your business plan then based on that information put together your Executive Summary. Let's us now move FORWARD and get ready for an actual pitch.▶

END OF EXECUTIVE SUMMARY SECTION

VI. Preparing An Elevator Pitch

This chapter will help you to understand how to properly organize your presentation and your thoughts. We will go over the elevator pitch vs. the full blown in person pitch in front of **a group of investors** or **a group of individuals** who have seen your business plan and are interested in hearing you speak about your opportunity.

THE ELEVATOR PITCH:

The elevator pitch is a very compact synopsis of what your project is all about that you can tell someone in **less than 45 seconds to a minute**. The following major headings are used for a very basic elevator pitch. They are the following:

1.   Call to action

2.   Why you?

3.   Why now?

4.   What/who?

They call it **"elevator pitch"** for a reason. It is a super quick synopsis and a great exercise to organize your thoughts.

Call to action: You can also think of this as your "**what if**" statement. Sample: What if I can provide a low cost, easy to use, super effective method that takes the place of tire chains in bad weather areas?

Why You?   Each year, extensive damage is done to city highways and local streets by the use of tire chains. Our solution causes no damage and is super effective in the traction it provides and the piece of mind it gives the driver in heavy storms.

Why Now? Being that we are trending towards more severe winter months, this amazing cloth tire covering will save city municipalities millions of dollars in damage and will help to prevent many an accident created by tires that cannot grip a slippery or icy surface.

What/Who? From the parent who takes their kids to school to the tractor trailer driver, our innovative easy to attach cloth tire cover will change the way every class of driver is able to cope for the better in heavy snowstorm areas.

So above is our **elevator pitch**. Notice, we gave the interested party 1) a very clear and concise overview of the project and we did it in a way that was 2) easy to grasp, easy to see why it is innovative, easy to understand 3) why it is unique and 4) exciting enough for a savvy business person to recognize the opportunity being presented.

THE EXPANDED ELEVATOR PITCH: PRACTICE WITH PASSION, ENERGY AND BE COMPELLING.

Finally, there is an **expanded version** of the **elevator pitch**. It is a bit more involved and might take an additional 30 to 45 seconds but it is worth exploring:

Call to Action: What if I can provide a low cost, easy to use, super effective method that takes the place of tire chains in bad weather areas?

Mission Statement: Our goal is to provide a low cost, easy to use cloth tire covering which is cost effective and damage free to highways when utilized in heavy snow fall areas.

Unique Differentiators: The current competition uses tire chains which are a hassle to put on but for the most experienced trucker and tire chains are known to break as well as cause damage to roadways that now can be a thing of the past due to our new product.

So What – Benefits: Our tire cover is easy to put on and easy to remove for the every day consumer to the professional. You don't have to be a mechanic in a gas station that grapples with tire chains. The comfort level that it gives the everyday driver as well as the professional trucker is priceless and the market price of $10.00 per pair cannot be beat.

Marketing Opportunity: Since this is a unique product we have the entire country to market to let alone Asia and Europe. This is a great ground floor opportunity that will afford us to market this product to every fleet, every gas station, every car supplies store, every car lot, every municipality, every place that sell autos, parts and tires of course. This is a wide open opportunity and the time to get involved is now. The product speaks for itself. This product "the cloth tire covering" is a welcome relief for a long standing problem.

Burning Problem: The problem that we currently face is alerting the public that the old solution of tire chains for heavy snow areas is an expensive and damaging method that is mainly utilized by truckers and other heavy vehicle operators while the vast majority of every day drivers struggle with their snow tires that do not always grip an icy or snow slick road thus jeopardizing their safety.

Tag Line: **Road Gripping Piece of Mind**

VII. The 12/20 Rule – Getting Ready To Get Ready

Now we come to the point where we are about to put together a slide show that we can take with us from meeting to meeting. We can unfold it as a slide show if we have an overhead projector or we can use paper copies of the slide show as well. Either way we are going to put together a slide show. You will know how it should professionally unfold and this will be of immense value to you. Keep in mind that you should be using **30 point font** on your slides and use bullets as much as possible to **highlight the main points** you are unfolding and avoid what they call **Tech Speak**. Most people are not up on **your** particular **industry jargon** so don't do it to impress because it could bore people and turn them off. Make sure you are speaking for a general audience rather than people specifically from your industry solely.

A couple of important things before we construct our slide show:

1. The **12/20 rule** refers to the **12 slides in 20 minutes** method that helps to keep your long pitch moving along smoothly. Remember, they normally let you do your pitch and if they feel that it interests them, they then will hit you with questions once the pitch is over.

2. Don't embarrass yourself as it relates to asking professional venture capitalists or professional angel investors to sign a non-disclosure agreement. They take it as an insult and they take it as a sign that you are clinging for life to the project and that your confidence and self esteem are weak. If you have done all you can to show that the project is clearly yours then relax and enjoy the process. If you have a **Trademark pending** or a **Provisional Patent**, **Domain Name**, **Social Media Names** locked down then relax. Believe me, if they see you have done your homework they will work with you. If you

have some shortcomings they might even step in and try to help you correct them if they are that enamored with your project.

3.	It is more important to have a viable concept and solid company than to think you are going to be handed millions of dollars. Very few high end venture capital deals are done each year in relation to how many deals are sent to venture capitalists. Most do not fit the criteria of being able to generate millions of dollars in profit. So, that does not mean that you give up. If you have a good idea then you use the business credit idea that I gave you, the crowd funding and other methods that I gave you and you and you may even try to get bridge loans in order to get past certain milestones but rest assured that if you have collateral, there are many hard money lenders out there if you can show them that an order for your goods exists, what you will profit from the order and that you will be able to pay their money back including their interest. Just to give you an idea of how many hard money lenders there are, go to Google and look up **Purchase Order Financing**, **Private Hard Money** and so on. There is money out there to help you to get going in one way or another.

4.	Some of you who have inventions and new business model projects might even attempt to get in with an **incubator**. An incubator will help you to get your business in proper order so that it can be properly funded. You should know that incubators will take a nice chunk of equity from your company but you will learn a lot, but just be aware that you can lose the control of your company in a way that you may or may not be comfortable with. Some people will *literally pay the price of less equity and control in order to be mentored* knowing that it is only their first project and there will be many more. This will help to build a resume, gain much needed experience and may open doors for future projects.

5.	For those of you that have a high level heavy duty new disruptive technology that will blow the lid off of an existing industry or create a new industry then **YES** you should target top venture capital firms. If you are smaller, then know that you can build your business piece by piece step by step. Does it matter if you grow to be very large in a few more years than originally thought? If you become a player, then venture capital people will no doubt take notice of you either way. You can build as fast or as slow as you are comfortable with. There are many ways to get exposure and test market your product or service. We have You Tube, Amazon Seller Central, Walmart, Ebay and on and on. Making use of You Tube and social media to spread the word with a little bit of an advertising budget will go a long way in getting you exposure.

6.   If you have a great business model idea then Franchising is another route you may wish to explore since it gives you the ability to expand using other people's money for each new store. The initial set-up will cost you money, but if it becomes popular and takes off, you can have let us say for example 500 stores open throughout the US and you then are the head of a large organization based on your franchised business model. Check out **Francorp.com** and **Entrepreneur.com** for a lot of free info on franchising a business concept.

7.   Before you go speak to anyone, your elevator pitch should be literally part of you and automatic and you should have **repeatedly practiced** your long 12 slide 20 minute pitch numerous times before you go in front of people. I read an interesting observation from Guy Kawasaki an entrepreneur where he said **"if you have the ability to pick a room, pick a room that's small and going to be crowded. Because, I would personally much rather speak to five-hundred people in a four-hundred fifty seat room than five-hundred people in a two-thousand seat room."** **"Yeah, it's more exciting, the chemistry is better, the emotion is better. Um, I would also recommend circulating with the audience prior to the speech so that you meet them and, you know, they form some kind of impression and bond with you so they want you to succeed as opposed to just hiding from the audience up to the very last minute like, you know, like musicians do."**

8.   **Guy Kawasaki's 10 most common lies from entrepreneurs.** I would like to list his 10 ten points and then give you my feedback. *1) Our projections are conservative, 2) Our market will be 50 billion by 2016, 3) Boeing will sign our contract next week, 4) Key employees will be joining as soon as we get funding, 5) No one else is doing what we do, 6) Several firms are doing due diligence on us, 7) Beta sites will pay to test our software, 8) Patents make our business defensible, 9) Microsoft is too slow to be a treat, 10) all we have to do is get 1% of the market*.

What these 10 most common entrepreneurial lies mean to venture capital people is that no one is going to make a major commitment to a concept that has not been backed by major money. So when the entrepreneur says no one else is doing what we do, perhaps they could have said after much research we have not been able to find any similar business model to date.

Making the broad **"no one is doing it"** statement is very hard to quantify and people who are looking to give money need total quantification. Saying a major entity **is to too slow to be a threat** -- well if they get wind about you with their major resources, **overnight** they can do what you want to do and knock you out, so you have to be careful what statements you make.

Look at the 10 carefully. What sounds like **bravado** in contrast to a statement that is **believable** and not **overbroad**. As to the patent question, it is always good to let them know that you have taken care of Intellectual Property issues but don't make the fact that you have or will have a patent or trademark the be all and end all. You can have a patent and a very poor team. You can have a patent or trademark and a bad business model etc. etc. etc.

9.   **Guy Kawasaki's 10 most common lies from venture capitalists.** Let us now look at the 10 most common lies that venture capital people are likely to tell you the money seeker. *1) We can make a quick decision, 2) I like your company but my partners didn't, 3) If you get a lead we will follow, 4) Show us some traction and we will invest, 5) We already have a lot of companies doing the same thing as you, 6) We are investing in your team, 7) We saw this coming so we didn't invest in B2B or B2C, 8) This is a vanilla term sheet, 9) We can open the doors for you at major companies, 10) We like early stage investing.*

Okay, so we take a look at the common lies or deceptions coming out of the venture capital side of things. What I get from them is that much of the 10 are designed to let you down easy. If they really like what you have, then they will let you know upfront and they are **not** going to let you walk and go to someone else who might make a windfall when they had you right there in front of them.

Other things that bother me are the following: The statement "**we already have a lot of companies doing the same thing as you**". That one in particular makes me suspicious and sounds to me like they have a contact in the industry and want you to feel that what you thought was unique is in fact already out there in force and you should drop your guard. **After all it is already out there right?.** This can be the furthest thing from the truth and don't believe it until you can confirm it!!! They may want to make a phone call to someone as soon as you leave to tell some other big company to jump on the concept knowing that you **do not** have the cash to fight. When it comes to new and innovative concepts you never know how money will affect someone.

Well, if you have a meeting and have done your research, and you feel that you have a unique concept and all of a sudden 3 months later you see it is now out there, I would be very suspicious of the guy who told you that we already have seen this numerous times. Make extensive and good notes no matter who you talk to or show your idea to. Number each and every Executive

Summary, Business Plan, slide show etc. with a unique numbering system and record who received what on what date and where it occurred. This will let the savvy venture capital guy know that you are keeping track of everything and it "**may**" make them think twice about doing something they may regret.

Another one that bothers me is "**this is a vanilla term sheet**". This one means the following. They are trying to get you to drop your guard and just sign on the dotted line. They are trying to get you to **not really read the fine print** of doing business with them and what you are going to lose in terms of equity and other decision making rights that you may not be comfortable with under the guise of we love your project just sign on the dotted line. **REMEMBER:** No term sheet from anyone is vanilla. Every firm had some lawyer (most probably from a major firm) who drafted some term sheet that gave **the overwhelming advantage** to the venture capital firm. Don't be so fast to sign anything. Don't be intimidated by any document either. Politely take the document and tell them **you will review it** and get back to them. If you have your own lawyer let them review it carefully. If you must do it yourself then you go line by line. If you don't understand a word then you look it up. Every document will have its own twists and turns. That is a guaranty. **Blacks Law Dictionary** whether you use the on-line version or the hard cover book will help you understand a lot of the legal terminology.

You must read everything to know all of the implications that this document will have and how it will affect your rights and your control over your project once you receive the funds they have promised. Remember, these guys for the most part think you are desperate and feel that it is only them who has brains so don't be so fast to kowtow. If they are actually going to fund you then you better believe it is because they know that your project is a possible winner. When you review their term sheet, you should feel free to make suggested corrections to the points and provisions that you are not comfortable with. You are not asking for the moon. You want to see if they are willing to negotiate on any of those items that you were not in total agreement with. I would suggest you make minor corrections not major corrections.

If they **will not** budge on the language in the document telling you it is a take it or leave it proposition, then you have to do some major soul searching because you most probably will lose a lot of your control and decision making ability. **You have to weigh the facts**. Is this going to be your only product? (Meaning this is it for me) Is this going to be one project of many that you will do? Maybe your name being associated with this project will open numerous doors on your other projects etc. and getting money for the next one will be that much easier, so think it over carefully and weigh the pros and cons. Get familiar with term sheets. You can download samples at the following locations: http://www.marsdd.com/articles/securing-investment-elements-of-a-term-sheet, techstartuplawyer.com (go to the Venture Capital Financing section), www.docracy.com and look for their term sheet guide.

VIII. Putting Together The Slide Show

We are going to be going over the nature of a **12 slide presentation**. Remember use size 30 Font. Go for **a predominantly bulleted format**. People don't like to read paragraphs. Now, they say that we should be starting off with the **last slide** first which is **"Why Us" Here is why you should invest with us**. Now, you could do this but, you can also go back to your **Elevator Pitch** and use the "**Call To Action**" statement that you had developed. I think this may be more effective and will immediately help to get people intrigued and to listen to what you have to offer. Remember, before you ever go before people practice this presentation at least 10 times. Perform it in front of family, friends, relatives and get their feedback but don't do it for the first time when it is going to really count. Don't blow an opportunity. Make sure you have thoroughly internalized the 12 slide presentation. So, let's do it! Not a bad idea to set up a website as well that generally talks about the project or industry along with some contact info and the ability to email you from that website.

Start with your "**Call to Action (What If)**" which you can take from your **Elevator Pitch**.

Slide 1:   <mark>Title</mark>: speaker intro & contact info; kick-off tag line. Whether you have an overhead projector or you hand out paper, have the above info on slide 1 and verbally introduce yourself with that same info to your audience. I am going to now take you through a mock 12 slide slideshow that will give you a decent idea of what you want to do when you present your concept. I purposely was not a concise as I could have been in the slides because I wanted you to see the thinking process involved.

Slide 2:   The Company: Overview of the company with the essence of your elevator pitch or a mission statement.

Slide 3:   **Players, Problem and Pain**: Market definition (who are the players); define the current problem and pain caused by the problem; include the market size.

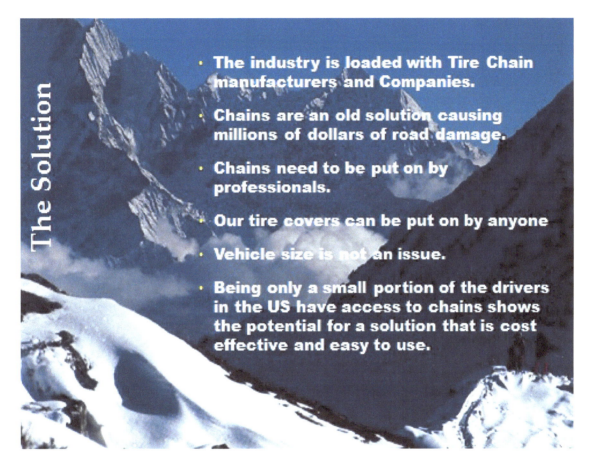

Slide 4:   **Pain Killer (i.e. Solution):** What do we bring to the table, how do we solve the problem, the benefits that are realized, the return on investment.

What We Bring To The Table

- Ease of use,
- Exponential Distribution to all auto related channels,
- Safety for the general public not just official vehicles,
- Heightened control on slippery roads.

- Distribution channels already in place,
- World wide interest,
- Life saving benefits,
- Great for cites that want to limit pothole damage,
- Tire covers that are easy to manufacture and work great on both ice and snow.

Comfort in bad weather...

Slide 5:   Technologies: "Our amazing intellectual property". If you have technology to offer give a brief overview. Stay away from tech speak but get your point across. If you don't have a new patent then talk about your great business model or your great service.

Slide 6:   **Competition**: Who else is doing this? (Don't forget status quo and home grown). So maybe you have competition but they don't do something the way you plan to which will make a major difference. How does your concept compare with the status quo.

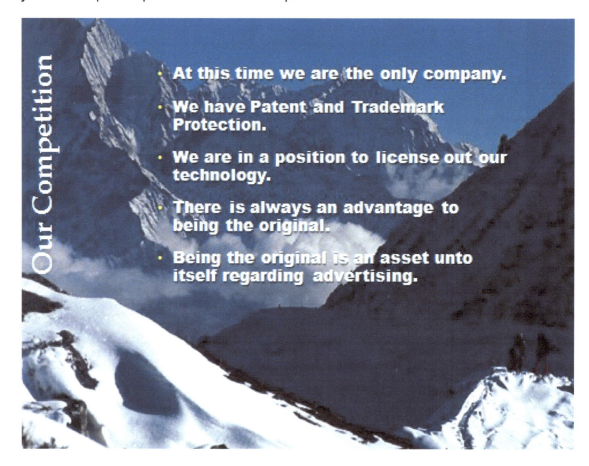

Slide 7:   **Business Model**:   Describe to the audience how we are going to make money.

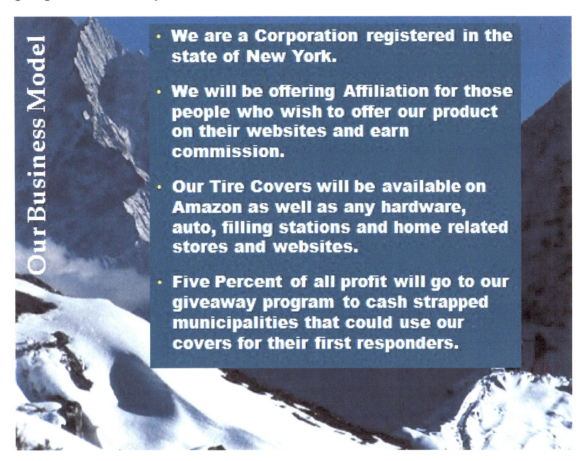

Our Business Model

- We are a Corporation registered in the state of New York.

- We will be offering Affiliation for those people who wish to offer our product on their websites and earn commission.

- Our Tire Covers will be available on Amazon as well as any hardware, auto, filling stations and home related stores and websites.

- Five Percent of all profit will go to our giveaway program to cash strapped municipalities that could use our covers for their first responders.

Slide 8: **Go To Market**: Your marketing plans. How do you plan to get the word out?

Slide 9: **Metrics and Money**: What will drive this business to revenue growth? Any margin projections?

What Will Lead To Profit

- We start out as the only cloth tire cover in the U.S.
- We already are well established in Europe.
- Municipalities will love the cost savings that occur due to damage to roadways from tire chains.
- Municipalities buy in bulk.

- Taxi fleets, truck fleets, etc. buy in bulk.
- Individuals buy for security on bad roads.
- Affiliates push our product to earn commissions.
- All distribution channels are already in existence.

Everyone benefits in some way...

Slide 10:   **Your Team**:   Brief overview of who will be responsible for your success.

Our Team

- **Walter Smith: Chief Engineer. Patent holder of 30 similar devices.**

- **Tom Smith: Marketing expert from ABC Corporation.**

- **John Smith: Distribution Expert from a top manufacturer.**

- **John Litigious: Intellectual Property attorney who oversees our Patent and Trademark issues and strategy.**

- **Bean Counter: Top CPA from the accounting firm of ABC Corp.**

- **Larsen Getalong: Public relations expert.**

Slide 11:   **Timelines and Status**: How you will use the money that is to be raised. Give an approximate timeline (can be multiple points) on how long it will take to hit certain milestones or to be up and running at the very least.

Timelines and Status

- We have borrowed 1 million dollars with a period of 5 years to pay back with 5% interest.
- We have 20,000 units ready to be sold.
- Large orders are backed by hard money lenders (Factors), based on our receivables.
- All profit goes back into the company making us less dependent on hard money.
- Profit margin increases steadily over a 1 year period.
- In year 2, we bring the company public which brings an infusion of cash eliminating the original loan.
- 30 Municipalities within the U.S. have pledged in writing to order our tire covers in bulk for the coming winter season.

Slide 12:   **The Wrap Up**: Here is why you should invest in us. You might end with the statement: If you should remember 3 things today: 1) Big point number 1, 2) Big point number 2 and 3) Big point number 3.

After you finish. Stay where you are and 1) welcome the room to ask you questions. 2) Make sure you have business cards. 3) If you have any type of sample whether **physica**l, **electronic prototype**, or **artist rendition** make sure you **display it prominently** at the meeting. 4) If there is an opportunity to grab everyone's business cards at the door or have them put down their email address on a clip board then do it. 5) There is nothing better than an on-point industry specific mailing list so don't lose a valuable opportunity. Always be growing your mailing list.

Some Angel, Venture Capital and Incubator sites to explore:
Angelcapitalcorporation.org, sterlingfunder.com, newyorkinvestmentnetwork.com, angel.co, gust.com, arcangelfund.com, newyorkangels.com, entrepreneur.com, soundboardangelfund.com, under30ceo.com, quora.com, bianys.com, nycedc.com, business-incubators.findthebest.com, dmoz.org, venturedeal.com, kpcb.com, greylock.com, usv.com, a16z.com, generalcatalyst.com

IX. Conclusion

If you have developed your Business Plan, Executive Summary, Elevator Pitch and 12/20 Slide Show, then you have a lot of essential and impressive information to be able to supply the various entities, acquaintances, possible partners, Angel Investors and the like that may just have interest.

Don't just hand all of your material to anyone that should inquire about your project! Start with the Executive Summary. Before you send it to anyone, have a numbering system that you keep so that everyone you have sent a copy to is carefully notated. Before you send anything, due your due diligence. Who runs this company? Take a look at the website, where are they located? Is the person you spoke to listed on the website? Who have they funded? Who are they connected with? You may opt to only send paper copies by mail, Fed Ex or Return Receipt Requested. If I can get away with not having to email things, I would rather do just that. I don't need people emailing my concept all over the place.

Some of you might opt to only meet people in person when you give out your materials. There is something to be said for in person meetings. Before you send things out, see if they are open to speaking face to face on **Zoom** or **Skype**. If they won't give you a few minutes face to face on-line then you can bet your concept will be one of many in a pile. You must respect yourself and what you bring to the table for others to properly respect you. If you truly have something of value, then the right person or entity at the right time will appear. Don't just send your project to everybody and anybody.

If you have a catchy name then you much check for Trademark availability and if available, grab your domain name, all social media that you can grab using that same name. This must be in place before you start distributing your materials.

Do not get discouraged if you don't find success immediately. If you believe in the project get out there and speak about it. Use the **radioguestlist.com** to set yourself up with as many interviews as possible. Use your elevator pitch. Don't give every secret away when you speak. Give enough to get interest but not enough for someone else to say "oh I get the whole picture" and try to end run you.

If you can't do it all at the beginning can you do a smaller version, can you do a mock version, can you do a smaller version that operates like the intended version, can you make use of local stores or businesses to allow you to implement your concept on a small scale so you can test it? At the very least, can you get an electronic prototype to show the vision and if a business model can it be run on a scale that lets you test the waters. If there is a will there is a way. If you need any help you can always call me or email me. If I can be of help, I certainly will try to make a difference. I do have some funding channels if your FICO is about 680 and above. I can help you to do a lot with minimal resources.

Regards,

Louis

www.lowcostempire.com